SEA TURTLES

NIGHTTIME ANIMALS

Lynn M. Stone

The Rourke Corporation, Inc.
Vero Beach, Florida 32964

Edited by Sandra A. Robinson

PHOTO CREDITS
All photos © Lynn M. Stone

Library of Congress Cataloging-in-Publication Data

Stone, Lynn M.
   Sea turtles / by Lynn M. Stone.
      p.   cm. — (Nighttime animals)
   Includes index.
   Summary: Examines the physical characteristics, habitats, and
behavior of sea turtles and describes some of the different kinds.
   ISBN 0-86593-296-4
   1. Sea turtles—Juvenile literature. [1. Sea turtles. 2. Turtles.]
I. Title. II. Series: Stone, Lynn M..Nighttime animals.
QL666.C536S775   1993
597.92—dc20   93-15691
                                                        CIP
                                                        AC

TABLE OF CONTENTS

SEA TURTLES

Sea turtles are the heavyweights of the turtle family. Some of them weigh hundreds of pounds.

Sea turtles live in parts of the oceans where the water is never very cold. There these **reptiles** face danger only from people and sharks.

Sea turtles spend nearly their whole lives in the ocean. Female sea turtles, however, come ashore to nest.

Most sea turtles nest only at night. The sea turtle crawls from the sea and picks her nest site on the dark beach.

A female sea turtle nests on a sandy beach away from waves, which could flood the nest

HOW SEA TURTLES LOOK

Like other turtles, sea turtles have their insides protected by a shell. The sea turtle's shell is streamlined and lightweight. Except for the leatherback's shell, sea turtle shells are hard. The leatherback sea turtle has a tough, leatherlike shell.

Unlike turtles of land and fresh water, sea turtles cannot "hide" their heads. Sea turtles have large shoulder muscles to power their long front flippers. The muscles leave no room for the head to withdraw into the shell.

Sea turtles have nowhere to hide their heads, but they rarely need to

KINDS OF SEA TURTLES

Most scientists say there are seven **species,** or kinds, of sea turtles. They are the green, hawksbill, loggerhead, olive ridley, Kemp's ridley, leatherback and flatback. All but the flatback are seen along American coasts at one time or another.

The only sea, or **marine,** turtle that nests in large numbers in the United States is the loggerhead.

The largest sea turtle is the leatherback. A 1,500-pound leatherback has been reported. Loggerheads usually weigh 170 to 350 pounds. Ridleys are the smallest marine turtles. They usually weigh about 80 pounds.

This loggerhead's "tears" will wash away sand and salt from her eyes while she lays her eggs

WHERE SEA TURTLES LIVE

In the United States, sea turtles are rarely found in the ocean north of New Jersey on the Atlantic coast. On the Pacific coast, they rarely swim north of California.

Sea turtles nest in the United States mostly along the coasts of North Carolina, South Carolina, Georgia and Florida.

Sea turtles sometimes stray into fairly cool ocean water during the summer.

The morning after nesting, the ocean tide begins to erase a sea turtle's trail on a Florida beach

A palm-sized baby loggerhead moments after hatching

A Florida State Parks ranger looks at a loggerhead egg at Sebastian Inlet State Recreation Area

WHAT SEA TURTLES EAT

Not all sea turtles eat the same things. Leatherbacks live almost entirely on jellyfish. Loggerheads eat jellyfish, too, but they prefer shellfish—crabs, for example. Both ridley turtles are also shellfish eaters.

The hawksbill eats marine plants and some animal life. Green turtles feed only on marine plants, including turtle grass.

Back at sea, marine turtles feed on plants and animals

NESTS IN THE NIGHT

On spring and summer nights, female loggerheads crawl from the ocean onto sandy, Southern beaches. The turtle uses her hind flippers like hands to dig a hole, her nest, in the sand. She lays about 110 moist, golf ball-sized eggs. She covers the hole with her hind flippers, and throws sand over her nesting place with her front flippers. Then she crawls back to the sea. Her trail looks like it might have been made by the treads of tractor tires.

A female loggerhead lays about 110 eggs in her nest hole

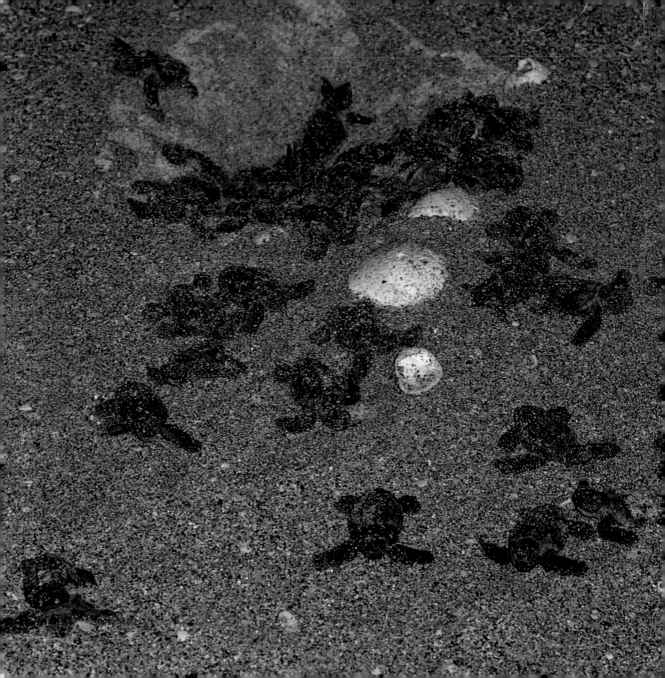

BABY TURTLES

Sea turtle eggs hatch about 10 weeks after they are laid. Each baby turtle is about the size of a silver dollar.

As soon as baby turtles pop out of their sand nest, they rush toward the ocean. Some built-in system sends them in the right direction.

Sea turtles hatch at night, when it is cool. At night, they are less likely to be attacked by **predators** such as herons and gulls. However, raccoons and ghost crabs catch some.

Just-hatched baby loggerheads stream from their nest on an August night

SEA TURTLE MYSTERIES

Female sea turtles have an amazing—and mysterious—ability. They often return to the beaches where they were hatched to lay their own eggs. This is called **"homing instinct."** How they locate their "home" beach is a mystery.

Another mystery is the age of a sea turtle when it begins to lay eggs.

Sea turtles probably live long lives, but no one knows how long. Scientists also don't know, for certain, the number of species of sea turtles.

Scientists know that marine turtles often nest on the shores where they were born

SEA TURTLES AND PEOPLE

Nearly all marine turtles are **endangered**—in danger of disappearing forever, becoming **extinct.** Kemp's ridley is in extreme danger, partly because it nests only on a few beaches along the Gulf of Mexico.

Sea turtles are protected by law along the coasts of the United States. In some other countries, however, people still hunt them for their meat, eggs, skins and shells. Sea turtles are victims of ocean pollution almost everywhere.

Glossary

endangered (en DANE jerd) — in danger of no longer existing; very rare

extinct (ex TINKT) — the point at which an animal species no longer exists

homing instinct (HO ming IN stinkt) — the natural ability of certain animals to return long distances to a home area

marine (muh REEN) — of or relating to the sea, salt water

predator (PRED uh tor) — an animal that kills other animals for food

reptile (REP tile) — the family of cold-blooded animals with backbones; alligators, crocodiles, snakes, turtles, lizards and tuatara

species (SPEE sheez) — within a group of closely-related living things, one certain kind or type (*loggerhead* turtle)

INDEX